*M*adison Foxcroft

**She Headhunter**

# *Book Club Supplement*

John Honeycutt

## $\mathcal{B}$ook Club Leader

$\mathcal{T}$hank you choosing Madison as a selection in your club. This supplement intends to assist you in facilitating discussion and better understanding some elements in the work which may have otherwise been less noticeable.

$\mathcal{M}$ay you and your group find insight, inspiration and self-discovery on your journey with Madison and the other characters.

***

# ❖ Story Arc

## *Original Creative Brief*

Madison Foxcroft, 33, leaves her position in a prestigious management consulting firm to join an elite all-female headhunting firm in New York. This publicly visible, but privately secret sisterhood finds and places individuals in various political, executive and leadership roles throughout the world. Their heritage reaches back centuries, when a woman's source of power often rested in her personal alliances and ability to help men advance into, or fall from a powerful position.

*** 

The next few sections illustrate the way three components were originally imagined to work together. Early on the "*soul, context,* and *intrigue*" were identified as separate, but inter-related parts of the story.

## *High Level Concepts*

𝒥his diagram ("Components of the Story") provided a basis for *compartmentalizing* the drafting of specific portions of the story. During the many iterations of the story-development, large portions – entire chapters even – did not make it to the final version. In some instances, detailed descriptions of scenes or events were collapsed into just a few sentences at the final draft. While difficult to *let-go-of*, the pieces discarded did not sufficiently lend themselves to the story as-a-whole. Pieces employed generally fit into one of these three component areas.

Components of the Story

Intrigue

3

Soul

1

Context

2

# *Soul*

*W*e shaped the soul of this story as "female journey" – which does not necessarily require a female protagonist. In this instance though, it is significant and intentional that the protagonist is female. Also the choice to develop the story as a *female journey* is equally significant and intentional.

Madison Foxcroft leaves a high-end management consultancy, Boone & McKinley, to join Echelon – an Executive Recruiting firm based in New York City.

Soul

Component #1 provides the "soul" of the story by introducing and engaging the reader to/with Madison, the main protagonist, as she experiences a "personal journey" in discovering herself as a woman.

| *F*emale Journey | *M*ale Journey |
|---|---|
| • *I*nternal journey | • *E*xternal journey |
| • *L*ots of peaks and valleys (mini-climaxes) throughout | • *L*ots to overcome … with one big climax at end |
| • *A*t end, protagonist proves himself or herself to himself or herself | • *A*t end, protagonist proves himself or herself to the world and others |
| • *T*he protagonist *gets or gains* himself or herself | • *T*he protagonist *gets* the girl (or the boy) |

## *Context*

$M$en thought women had no need for education or the ability of public speaking. Their role mostly consisted of taking care of their kids and taking care of a house. The role of women was fought over in France for over several centuries. There were arranged marriages at as young as fifteen years old. Some women were rulers or became authors, but it was not common. Some questions we considered:

- $H$ow might a woman have gained power during this era?

- $H$ow might those ways be similar or differ-from today?

A "sister-hood" or secret society of women is formed around the 13th-16th centuries in Europe. The group exerts influence in their world by assisting men in gaining powerful positions, or falling from those positions.

Component #2 provides the "context", or the historical back-story, of Echelon – which remains a modern day secret sisterhood – but also has a modern day "front" of being an executive recruiting firm.

2      Context

*9*

## *Intrigue*

𝒯he portions resulting in large pieces left on the cutting-room floor came from here. The intrigue required a sufficient level of detail to move Madison through her journey, but not so much as to *become* the story itself. Alicia, Paul, Malena, Dr. Bacher, and other secondary characters are instrumental in telling the *intrigue* portions of this journey. Madison's girl friends, Axel, and Eaton are not contributors to the intrigue; rather they support soul-finding elements. Elizabeth, Helena and Lola are part of both (e.g., support for the intrigue and soul).

3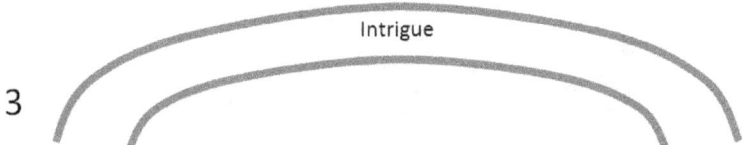

The intrigue centers on a modern-day issue of human-trafficking out of Latin America. The protagonist, Madison, becomes engaged in helping address aspects of this horrific issue through her job at Echelon ... but more significantly following her *induction* and acceptance into the "sisterhood".

Component #3 provides the over-arching conflict to the story which facilitates the pace – and emotional responses from the reader.

# ❖ Literary

# *Discussion Opportunities*

## Literary Devices in this Work

Each of these are used at least one time in this body of work. A few are used multiple times. As a potential activity – *as a group or as individuals* – identify portions of the book which make use of these devices.

- *Allusion* is a reference to something literary, mythological, or historical that the author(s) assume the reader will recognize.

- *Epiphany* a moment of sudden realization or insight.

- *Euphemism* an indirect, less offensive way of saying something that is considered unpleasant, improper or for humorous/dramatic impact.

- *Flash forward* (and *flashback*) is a scene that takes the narrative forward or backward in time from the current point of the story.

- *Foil* is when two or more characters highlight each other by their differences (*e.g., heroine and villain*).

- *Foreshadowing* is often described as a literary device which *hints* toward what is to come.

- *Free verse* poetic form that does not have a regular meter or rhyme scheme.

- *Imagery* when the writer or speaker uses their descriptions to access the senses of the reader of listener.

- *Irony* a contrast between what is expected and what actually exists or happens.

- *Juxtaposition* placing two elements side by side to present a comparison or contrast. (*Hint: the school*).

- *Onomatopoeia* when the words sound like what they mean. (*One example: "blap"*).

- *Personification* representing an abstract quality or idea as a person or creature.

- *Pun* is a play on words, often achieved through the use of words with similar or identical sounds but different meanings.

- *Red herring* is used to describe elements intended to mislead the audience or reader.

- *Side shadowing* is the practice of including scenes that turn out to have no relevance to the primary plot but may serve to better emulate reality.

- *Symbol* something that stands for or represents something else.

\*\*\*

*Others: Allegory, Alliteration, Amplification, Anagram, Analogy, Anastrophe, Anecdote, Anthropomorphism, Antithesis, Aphorism, Archetype, Assonance, Asyndeton, Authorial Intrusion, Bibliomancy, Bildungsroman, Cacophony, Caesura, Characterization, Chiasmus, Circumlocution, Conflict, Connotation, Consonance, Denotation, Diction, Doppelganger, Ekphrastic, Epilogue, Epithet, Euphony, Hubris, Hyperbaton, Hyperbole, Internal Rhyme, Inversion, Kennings, Litotes, Malapropism, Metaphor, Metonymy, Mood, Motif, Negative Capability, Nemesis, Oxymoron, Paradox, Periodic Structure, Periphrasis, Plot, Point of View, Polysyndeton, Portmanteau, Prologue, Satire, Setting, Simile, Stanza, Stream of consciousness, Suspense, Synecdoche, Synesthesia, Syntax, Theme, Tone, Tragedy, Understatement, Verisimilitude, Verse.*

# ❖ Cast

## *Quick Stats*

### Top Mentions Quiz

The top mentioned characters in rank order are:

| | |
|---|---|
| Madison | 371 |
| Alicia | 208 |
| Elizabeth | 130 |
| Malena | 98 |
| Isabelle | 91 |
| Paul | 46 |
| Axel/Axie | 46 |

### Animals with Names

Axel (mutt)          Seal (horse)

### Heroine / Villain

Madison Foxcroft >>     << Dr. Reiner Bacher
Isabelle >>          << Desidario
Malena Juarez >>        << Eduardo

### Doppelganger (sort-of)

Nancy Cartwright >>     << Sylvia Cartwright

# *Quick Facts*

## Madison's Girlfriend Quiz

*M*adison's girl friends (at birthday celebration):

| | |
|---|---|
| Patrice | Married to Marcus |
| Leigh | College best friends |
| Melody | Good friend |

## Madison's Men Quiz

*M*adison's potential dates or relationships:

| | |
|---|---|
| Billy | Umm, no ("y") |
| Darryl | Nice, but no sparks |
| No Name Given | Volkswagen lover |
| Price | Past boyfriend/married |
| Eaton | Fireman/met online |
| Paul | Elizabeth's youngest |

## Madison's Echelon Co-workers

*M*adison's primary co-workers at Echelon:

| | |
|---|---|
| Elizabeth Oskmey | CEO |
| Alicia | Queen of office |
| Lola | Wears no make-up |
| Helena | Miss Peachtree |

## *Primary Segment Characters*

### Isabelle

*I*sabelle's community:

| | |
|---|---|
| Isabelle | & Mattias Kohl |
| Johanna (Bruder) | & Hans |
| Adelheid (Bruder) | & Niklas |

*I*sabelle's inquisition moments:

| | |
|---|---|
| Hans | Stephan |
| Jacob | Desidario |
| Father Peter | |

*I*sabelle's Ireland:

| | |
|---|---|
| Cillian O'Donnchadhas | Maeve |
| Margaret Fitzpatrick | Lady Keighley |

### Malena Section

| | |
|---|---|
| Papi | Malena's father |
| Eduardo | Lead recruiter |
| Carlos | Recruiter |
| Valencia | New friend |
| Wile E. Coyote | Transportation |

# ❖ Backstage

# Author's Early Collaboration

## For Your Interest

---

The authors, John and Faryn, connected through a crowd-sourcing web site. The two completed this work without having met, and with only one phone call. All collaboration and exchange was conducted through email only. As of the date of publication (February 2016), the authors have not yet met in person.

To launch the collaboration, a set of "one-pagers" provided guidance to the authors, keeping their perspectives aligned. Here is a subset of the documents:

## Documents library

Concept Documents

- SH01_Management_Consulting.pdf
- SH02_Executive_Recruiting.pdf
- SH03_Perspective_Men__Women.pdf
- SH04_Early Europe.pdf
- SH05_New_York_City.pdf
- SH06_Shoes.pdf
- SH07_Culture.pdf
- SH08_Female_Journey.pdf
- SH09_Dominate.pdf
- SH10_Flesch-Kincaid.pdf
- SH11_Year 2010 computer bug.pdf
- SH16 - Crime Stoppers.pdf
- SH17 - Project Management.pdf
- SH18 - Regime Change.pdf
- SH19 - Herbal Potions.pdf
- SH20 - Latin America.pdf

*Not all aspects originally outlined in the one-page summaries made it to the final book. However, this approach, along with the over-arching framework described at the front of this booklet, kept the authors focused. Below, find extracts from the original one-page documents. These provide some insight to how the collaboration process unfolded.*

00. Madison Foxcroft, 33, leaves her position in a prestigious management consulting firm to join an elite all-female headhunting firm in New York. This publicly visible, but privately secret sisterhood finds and places men in various political, executive and leadership roles throughout the world. Their heritage reaches back centuries, when a woman's source of power often rested in her personal alliances and ability to help men advance into, or fall from a powerful position.

01. Management Consulting is a broad phrase used to express a variety of professional services. In general, there are a few major sub-groupings for management consulting: Information Technology consulting – also called IT; Strategic consulting – often provided at the Boardroom level – or at the "C-Suite" which is a new way of saying "executive suite." The "C" in C-Suite indicates "Chief" ... as in Chief Financial Officer, and Chief Marketing Officer; Business process improvement – sometimes called "BPI" – or process re-engineering which became in-vogue during the 1990's; Several forms of strategy and planning – including marketing strategy, technology strategy, location strategy, human resources strategy.

02. Headhunting is the industry expression for executive recruiting. Madison leaves Boone & McKinley to join an executive search/recruiting firm. There are thousands of small ("single shingle") firms/shops around the country (US). There are "tiers" of such agencies ... at the very lowest end, these might be called "body shops" ... where somewhat generic or "commodity" skills – are provided to a client at a small fee – ranging possibly from $1,000 per placement up to $10,000 per placement. At the

middle-upper tier – there are two types of searches – an "exclusive retained search" is the most lucrative. These will "source" (meaning search) for specific set of "talent" that fits a client organization's culture. Often the agency will present only 2 or 3 candidates – possibly as many as 5 or 6 … but that would be unusual … at the very top of the food-chain, a Board of Directors … or only the most senior-most executives will then interview and get to know the candidates identified from the Agency. The Agency will have provided a significant background check – and verification. Fees are highly negotiable on these deals from the client organization and the agency … but they would typically range from 20% of the annual compensation of the recruited executive up to 40%. The agency (on an exclusive retained search) would get a commission regardless of whether or not they found and placed a target candidate into the role.

03. This information below would not be agreed-upon by all people. A specific resource that is interesting and to-a-degree, a basis of this fiction work … is the exploration that men and women do have very different needs and expectations of each other … in spite of modern-day political correctness. A book "His Needs – Her Needs" – and widely popular several years ago for married people listed a basic premise is that there are five "Her Needs" and five "His Needs" …everyone "needs all ten" … but that's not the point … the point is that woman are drawn the five … and men to a different five.

04. This book should not over-do it on historical premise … but the Headhunting firm does have "roots" in some sort of "sister-hood" or sorority that may date back to the 14th-15th century – Europe in particular. This was a time of "reformation" and change …

05. New York City.

06 Madison is a "shoe aficionado" ... this is somewhat of a cliché thing (in media) for some upwardly mobile New York female professionals. Even so, Madison has fallen prey: Christian Louboutin, Jimmy Choo, and Steve Madden. But beyond this, the notion that shoes tell you something about the person is an interesting study in behavior and culture. Nobles wore shoes that made them taller than their subjects ... sometimes overtly, and sometimes under a dress or gown or robe so that the additional height couldn't readily be recognized.

07. Culture as defined by Webster's (paraphrased) is attitudes, assumptions, and behavior ... or a belief system of an individual or group of individuals.

Anthropologists and Archeologists attempt to understand and describe a culture through the set of observed artifacts ... symbols, ceremonies, rituals, celebrations, and customs.

Modern day culture (US) has a set of collective attitudes, assumptions and behaviors ... and we also have a shared set of symbols, ceremonies, rituals, celebrations and customs.

For example:

☐ We celebrate birthdays

☐ We give driver's licenses to 16 year-olds

☐ We have graduation ceremonies

☐ We give gold watches to retirees

☐ We set aside the 4th of July

Less obvious until you think about it:

☐ Some men wear jackets and ties – others don't

☐ A flick of the hair from a woman can be flirting

☐ Certain music is deemed more appropriate than other music in various situations

☐ The volume of voice is an indirect way of "saying something"

Without over-doing it, the concepts of culture would be appropriate to identify and incorporate into the story … the word "culture" might never be used … but let's challenge ourselves with how to weave in concepts of culture to observations and dialogue between the characters.

08. Most of us are aware of … and able to recognize... a "Guy Movie" and a "Chick Flick". this story should be more of a chick-flick than a guy movie. But the following may help describe the differences:

Both guy and chick movies might have a male or female protagonist. In this instance the fact that the protagonist Madison happens to be a female does not in itself make it a "chick" or female journey. These are the attributes to achieve:

☐ Internal journey – enabled through the external

☐ Lots of peaks and valleys

☐ Madison proves herself to herself (self-validation)

09. This story should not be centered on this subject – but it should be inclusive of the subject through the character of Alicia. Consideration: Madison's naivety – although a grown woman with a lot of "business" real-world experience, will be uncomfortable with the subject and learn something about herself and others (men and woman) during this part of her journey.

10. Generally speaking, this text should target an average Flesch-Kincaid Grade level reading index of 11.5 to no more than 12.5.

11. Base this loosely on the actual historical events. A "tech-Geek" plants a series of bugs in banking system computers over ten years prior to the 2010 event in Europe. He does this while having access to banking system computers during his time programming and correcting for the Y2K bug.

12-15 Not shown here.

16. This may only play a very small part in the story – still having the nuances correct will be important. Regardless, the primary scene that uses the concept of crime stoppers is when the tech-geek "turns himself in" – but disclosing himself as a thief to a waitress who can then use the reward money to pay some college tuition.

17-18. Not shown here.

19. A "packet of salt" or something similar will be "slipped" to the Tech-Geek while he is in the North portion of Riker's Island jail. This will temporarily slow his metabolism until he appears to have little or no pulse and other vital signs. It will be following this that the Sisters retrieve him in an ambulance – and subsequently "replace" him with an actual recently dead corpse. It's the John Doe they deliver to the actual hospital – whereas he is pronounced dead on arrival.

In truth though, the Tech Geek will recover under the care of the Sisters – so that he can continue to participate in the intrigue portion of the story.

Possibly, other small segments of the book can draw from "potions" of one sort or another – that have a long-lived heritage, passed down through the ages in the sisterhood. While it will be okay to have a glancing nod to mysticism from perhaps one of the Sisters – the remaining will view the potions (while secret) simply as euphoric drugs or similar in many ways to modern-day drugs (i.e., not Magic). The book and the Sisterhood are not about mysticism – even if some of their early heritage is rooted in this.

Potions should not be a centerpiece of the book – but rather gently woven in as a natural complement to the heritage of where the group came from.

20. Not shown here.

# ❖ Discussion

## *Facilitator Questions*

### Adapt These to Your Book Club

1. *R*eview the differences between a female and male journey (see the "Soul" section of this facilitator's guide). How well did this book achieve a "female journey?"

2. *D*escribe Madison, Isabelle, and Malena in terms of their respective personality traits, motivations, and inner qualities. Which traits are similar?  Which are different?

3. *D*escribe Madison in terms of personal growth from the beginning of the book compared to the end. Does she learn something about herself?

4. *I*s the plot engaging—does the story interest you? Were you surprised by the plot's complications?

5. *D*iscuss the book's structure. Do the authors use a single viewpoint or shifting viewpoints? Why might the authors have chosen to tell the story the way they did—and what difference does it make in the way you read or understand it?

6. *W*hat symbols are used to describe or reinforce a scene, event, or individual?

7. *W*hen comparing the opening and closing passages, what strikes you about the similarities and differences?

8. *I*s the ending satisfying? If so, why? If not, why not...and how would you prefer it to end?

9. *I*s there an inspiration or a personal learning discovered in this work? If you could ask John or Faryn a question, what would you ask?

10. *H*as this novel changed you? Has it broadened your perspective? Have you been challenged to alter your way of thinking or an action you might choose to take?

# ❖ Consider

## *Current Women's Topics and Issues*

*D*ozens of potential women-centric topics exist. Some of these were raised in the book. Some were included directly as part of the story – others mentioned only with an oblique reference. Consider using this list to discuss the book itself, and possibly the topic category in general.

### Quick List

| Direct Topic | Less Direct |
|---|---|
| Children (having/caring) | Catcalling |
| Domestic violence | Closing the pay gap |
| Intersectionality | Family-leave policies |
| More women into tech | Gender pay gap |
| Recognizing real bodies | LGBTQ rights |
| Trafficking/sex trade | Reproductive rights |
| Violence against women | Stalking and harassment |

\*\*\*

*Others contemporary topics not directly or indirectly included in this book: Breastfeeding; Female genital mutilation (FGM); Low rape conviction rate; Racial Justice; Sex-selective abortions; Trolling; Women in (political) office.*

## Human Trafficking Estimates

*A*n estimated 2.5 million people are in forced labour (including sexual exploitation) at any given time as a result of trafficking. According to UN.GIFT, of these:

- 1.4 million (56%) are in Asia and the Pacific
- 250,000 (10%) are in Latin America
- 230,000 (9.2%) are Middle East & N. Africa
- 130,000 (5.2%) are in sub-Saharan countries
- 270,000 (10.8%) are in industrialized countries
- 200,000 (8%) are in countries in transition

\*\*\*

*O*ver 160 countries are reported to be affected by human trafficking by being a source, transit or destination.

\*\*\*

For additional book club and other support, visit

**MadisonFoxcroft.com**

www.ingramcontent.com/pod-product-compliance
Lightning Source LLC
Chambersburg PA
CBHW071321280526
45788CB00004B/1977